THE SOUTHWEST

by Sarah Glasscock

Table of Contents

Introduction

You'll find the hottest desert in America in the Southwest. In the summer, it can get as hot as 105 degrees. But in April, if you visit the Sonoran Desert, you might find snow on the ground.

The world's tallest fountain is in Arizona. Water shoots 560 feet in the air. It's 90 degrees outside. The water feels great.

Or you can go to cool caves in Texas. It's always about 70 degrees in the Natural Bridge Caverns.

The Southwest is the hottest and driest **region** in the United States. Arizona, New Mexico, Colorado, Texas, and Oklahoma make up this region.

What Is a Region?

A region is a large area made up of places that share some features. These features include geography and climate. The people in a region share their history, too. And they often share how they make a living.

In this book, you'll learn about the geography and climate of the Southwest region. You'll also learn a little about the history of the region. And last, you'll find out how people live there today.

▼ The Natural Bridge Caverns are near San Antonio, Texas.

Geography and Climate

The states in the Southwest share natural features. Two great rivers—the Rio Grande and the Colorado—run through part of the region. This chapter is about the **landforms** in the Southwest. You'll also find out about the region's sunny and warm climate.

Forests

The Southwest has thirty-one national forests. Many of the forests cover more than one million acres of land. Think about how much room one million football fields would take up. That's how big one million acres is.

Forest fires are a danger in the spring and summer. A careless camper or lightning can spark a fire.

4

Deserts

The Sonoran (suh-NOR-uhn) Desert covers parts of Arizona. This desert is the only place the giant saguaro (suh-WAHR-oh) cactus grows. Hawks and other birds nest in the cactuses. Jackrabbits and mule deer also eat saguaros.

The Chihuahuan (chuh-WAH-wahn) Desert covers an area of 196,700 square miles. It covers parts of Texas, Arizona, and New Mexico. The Rio Grande runs through the Chihuahuan Desert. You might spot the Rio Grande frog in the river.

Solve This #1

Only one southwestern state—Texas—has a larger area than the Chihuahuan Desert. The area of Texas is 268,601 square miles. About how much larger in area is Texas than the Chihuahuan Desert?

Math ✔ Point

What information from the text did you need to solve the problem?

5

Mountains

There are many **mountain ranges** in the Southwest. The largest mountain range is the Rocky Mountains. The Rockies are more than 3,000 miles (4,800 kilometers) long. They stretch from northern Mexico all the way to Alaska.

Many of the mountains in Colorado are taller than 14,000 feet (4,267 meters). These mountains are nicknamed "Fourteeners." There are fifty-four "Fourteeners" in Colorado. The tallest is Mt. Elbert. It is 14,431 feet (4,399 meters) high. You will find Fourteeners in other states as well. California has twelve, Washington has two, and Alaska has sixteen.

▲ Long's Peak is one of Colorado's "Fourteeners." It is 14,259 feet (4,346 meters) high. Climbing the peak can be a real adventure.

▲ Fort Union, New Mexico, is on the western edge of the Great Plains. It was on the Santa Fe Trail.

Plains

The Great Plains are east of the Rocky Mountains. These **plains** reach into parts of Oklahoma, Colorado, Texas, and New Mexico. The plains are a grassland region. Early Native Americans of the Great Plains hunted the buffalo, or bison, that lived there.

Then settlers began to move west. Some took the Santa Fe Trail to New Mexico. You can still see the ruts from their wagon wheels on the old trail.

Elevation

The **elevation**, (eh-luh-VAY-shuhn) or height, of the thirteenth step of Colorado's state capitol building in Denver is exactly 5,280 feet (1,609 meters). We use elevation as a measuring tool. If you start from sea level, which is 0 feet, the step is one mile above sea level.

The elevation along the Texas Gulf Coast is 0 feet. That makes sense since a **gulf** is part of a sea.

It's a Fact

Santa Fe is the capital of New Mexico. At 7,000 feet (2,133 meters) above sea level, Santa Fe is the highest capital city in the United States.

▼ Santa Fe, New Mexico

You can view stars and planets through large telescopes in the Southwest. The telescopes are in observatories on top of mountains.

▲ Kitt Peak Observatory in Arizona is at an elevation of 6,875 feet (2,095 meters).

Solve This #2

a. Suppose you drive from the lowest point in Arizona to the highest point in New Mexico. How many feet in elevation would you climb?

b. Then you drive to the highest point in Colorado. How many feet in elevation would you climb?

State	Lowest Elevation (in feet)	Highest Elevation (in feet)
Arizona	70 Colorado River	12,633 Humphreys Peak
Colorado	3,315 Arikaree River	14,433 Mt. Elbert
New Mexico	2,817 Red Bluff Lake	13,161 Wheeler Peak
Oklahoma	287 Little River	4,973 Black Mesa
Texas	0 (sea level) Gulf of Mexico coast	8,749 Guadalupe Peak

9

Precipitation

The Southwest is dry. It gets less **precipitation** (pree-sih-puh-TAY-shuhn) than any other region in the United States. But heavy rains can hit the region and cause floods.

▲ **Heavy rains fall across the Southwest in summer.**

From July to September, heavy rains often hit the Southwest. The storms are called **monsoons**.

Snow and ice fall in the region, too. People go to the mountains of Arizona, Colorado, and New Mexico to ski.

Average Precipitation in the Southwest

Precipitation (in inches)

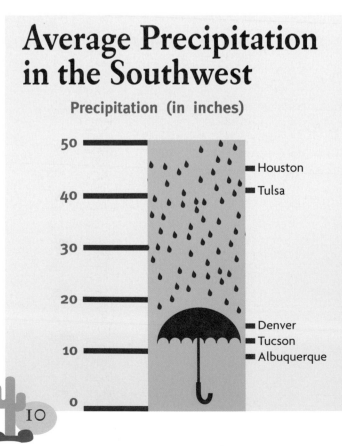

Solve This #3

Use the table to answer the questions.
a. About how much precipitation does Tulsa get in a year?
b. What is the range of rainfall for the five cities? (Remember: The difference between the least number and the greatest number is the range.)

Temperature

Have you ever tried to fry an egg on a hot sidewalk? If you lived in Phoenix, you might. The temperature often shoots up to 100 degrees or more! You can cook an egg on a sidewalk that is about 145 degrees. But does this ever happen? So far, June 26, 1990, has been the hottest day ever in Phoenix. The temperature hit 122 degrees!

▼ Phoenix, Arizona

☑ Point

Make Connections

Use the internet site www.weather.com to locate the average temperature in your city or town. How does it compare to Phoenix?

Chapter 2

The People

Many groups of people live in the Southwest. Those groups have moved into the region at different times in history.

Native Americans

Native Americans were the first people to reach the Southwest. They have lived in the region for thousands of years.

◀ Native Americans built their homes in the sides of cliffs. Montezuma Castle in Arizona is five stories tall. It was built about 700 years ago.

Apache, Cherokee, Hopi, Navajo, and Pueblo are some of the tribes that still live in the region.

Today there are nineteen Pueblo communities in New Mexico. Their square houses are made of **adobe** (uh-DOH-bee) bricks. The bricks are made from earth, straw, and water. They are dried in the sun.

The Pueblo are talented artists. They make beautiful pottery, jewelry, and rugs. During the year, they celebrate traditional feast days with singing and dancing. The songs and dances have been passed down for hundreds of years.

▼ A Pueblo house has adobe walls several feet thick. This keeps the house cool in the heat.

They Made a Difference
Navajo Code Talkers

The Navajo language is only spoken in small areas of Arizona and New Mexico. It is not a written language. This makes it perfect for sending secret messages. So, in World War II, the Marines used Navajo soldiers to send and receive secret messages. The soldiers spoke to each other in Navajo over the radio. The enemy was never able to understand the messages.

13

Some Indian nations came to the Southwest less than 200 years ago. In the 1830s, settlers wanted more and more land in the Southeast. So the United States set up the Indian Territory, now Oklahoma. The Southeastern nations were forced to move to the Southwest.

16,000 Cherokee had to walk over 1,000 miles to the Indian Territory on the Trail of Tears.

Native Americans Living in the Southwest

State	Population in 2000
Arizona	255,879
Colorado	44,241
New Mexico	173,483
Oklahoma	273,230
Texas	118,362

Solve This #4

The table to the left shows the Native American population in the Southwest in 2000. Which state has the biggest Native American population? What is the average population?

Math Point

What information did you need to solve this?

The Spanish Arrive

In the 1500s, the Spanish came to the Southwest. They hoped to find gold and other riches. They wanted to claim land for Spain, too. Most of the Spanish settled near the Rio Grande.

Trouble often broke out between the Native Americans and the Spanish. The Spanish wanted to take the Indians' land. They also wanted the Indians to work for them. But they did not want to pay the Native Americans.

It's a Fact

A Spanish explorer, or conquistador [kahn-KEES-tah-dawr] might wear up to eighty pounds of metal, including a helmet and a sword.

▲ Explorer Hernando de Soto was a conquistador.

The Spanish changed the Southwest. They brought cattle, sheep, and horses to the region. Soon the Native Americans began to raise cattle and sheep. They also started to ride horses. The Spanish brought the rodeo with them to the New World. The first rodeos were held in the Southwest in the 1600s.

It's a Fact

A special rodeo is held in Texas and New Mexico. It is called *la charreada* [LAH chah-REE-ah-dah]. This kind of rodeo started in Mexico. Riders wear fancy costumes. Music plays a big part.

Farmers, Ranchers, and Miners

During the 1800s, the United States grew very fast. Many people headed west. They wanted land for farms and ranches. Some of them also hoped to find gold. Many settled in the Southwest.

The Indian Territory in Oklahoma was first set up for Native Americans only. But as the country grew, settlers wanted more land. Soon the Indian Territory was opened to non-Indian settlers. Once again, the Indians had to move.

The Oklahoma Land Rush

On the morning of April 22, 1889, two million acres of Oklahoma territory were opened to settlers. The land had been part of the Indian Territory. So many people rushed in on that morning that the ground shook.

▲ the Oklahoma land rush, 1891

17

▲ Juneteenth celebration in California

▲ Nat Love was known as Deadwood Dick.

Many African Americans took part in the Oklahoma Land Rush. Most had once been enslaved. After the Civil War, they could own land. Towns founded by freed slaves grew up in Oklahoma. Many of the towns still exist.

African Americans founded Boley, Oklahoma, as an all-black town in 1903. Today, about 1,100 people live in Boley. The town is home to the oldest African American rodeo in the country. Every summer, thousands of people come to see the town and watch the rodeo.

Primary Source

In 1863, all the slaves in the United States were freed. The news didn't reach African Americans in Texas until June 19, 1865. Former slave Felix Hayward described that day: "Everybody went wild . . . We were free. Just like that, we were free." Today, June 19, known as Juneteenth, is celebrated across the Southwest and other regions.

18

Settlers discovered that the Southwest was rich in minerals. People found coal, gold, silver, and copper. Many Southwestern towns grew up around mines. When the mines were used up, people left. The towns became ghost towns.

Today you can visit the ghost towns. One ghost town is Independence, Colorado. It grew up near a gold mine. In 1882, 1,500 people lived there. Then less and less gold was found in the mine. Soon almost everyone had left Independence.

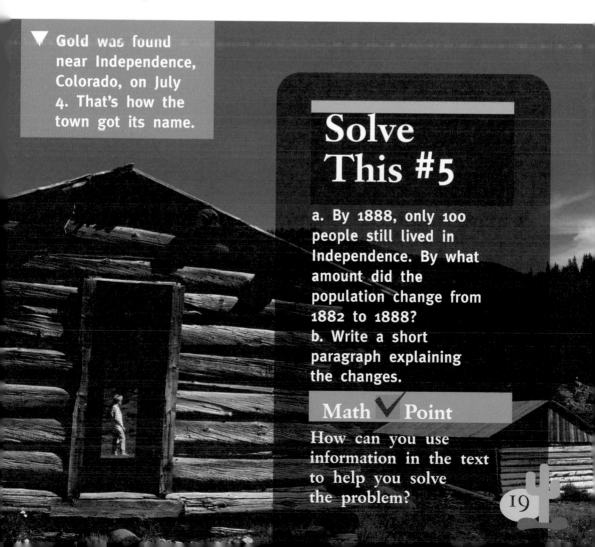

▼ Gold was found near Independence, Colorado, on July 4. That's how the town got its name.

Solve This #5

a. By 1888, only 100 people still lived in Independence. By what amount did the population change from 1882 to 1888?

b. Write a short paragraph explaining the changes.

Math ✔ Point

How can you use information in the text to help you solve the problem?

The Southwest Today

The population of the Southwest is growing. One reason is the warm climate. People move there to find jobs, too. They use the land and the region's natural resources to earn a living.

Balloons aren't the only things that fly over Albuquerque. Every fall, flocks of sandhill cranes and Canadian geese arrive, too. They spend the winter there.

Where People Live

Some of the people in the Southwest live in small towns, like Marfa, Texas. Ranching was once the town's main business. Many artists now live there. Visitors come from all over the world to see the art in Marfa.

Albuquerque, New Mexico, is a fast growing city. In 1990, about 350,000 people lived there. Today, almost 500,000 people live in the city. People move to Albuquerque because of the sunny, dry climate.

Visitors also enjoy the city. Each fall, Albuquerque holds a balloon **festival**. Large, colorful hot air balloons float above the city.

▼ El Paso, Texas, has an average of 200 sunny days every year.

21

Denver, Colorado, was founded in 1858 by gold miners. It's known as the Mile-High City. Can you guess why? Turn back to page 8 to find out. Like Albuquerque, Denver is growing fast. In 1990, about 470,000 people lived there. Today, about 560,000 people live in Denver.

The Denver Mint

The Denver Mint makes U.S. coins. It opened in 1863. Miners used to take their gold to the Denver Mint. The mint paid the miners for their gold. Then the gold was melted and turned into bars.

▼ Denver, Colorado

Solve This #6

What is the elevation of Denver in yards? (Remember that one mile = 5,280 feet).

Math ✔ Point

Explain how you changed a mile into yards.

Art in the Southwest

Artists have always been drawn to the beauty of the
Southwest. The photographer Ansel Adams was born in
San Francisco in 1902. He spent much of his career taking
pictures in the Southwest. His black-and-white photographs
have become symbols of the American wilderness. This photo
of a moonrise in Hernandez, New Mexico, was taken in 1941.

How People Earn a Living

The Southwest's sunny climate draws many businesses. Tourists on vacation enjoy its beauty and warm climate.

Mining still goes on in Arizona and Colorado. Arizona produces about two-thirds of America's copper. Texas **exports** more products than any other state. It makes and ships chemicals, leather, and computers to other countries.

▼ The roof of Arizona's capitol building is made of copper. It has about as much copper as 4,800,000 pennies!

24

Instead of crops, some people in the Southwest produce energy. Ranchers and farmers have long used windmills to pump water. Today wind farms produce electricity for many towns and cities.

They Made a Difference

Michael Dell was a student at the University of Texas at Austin. He had a new idea and started a company in his dormitory room. He sold his computers directly to customers, not through stores. Today Dell Computers is one of the biggest computer companies in the world.

Another major industry in the region is space. Astronauts train at the Johnson Space Flight Center in Houston, Texas. And many of the first rockets have been tested in New Mexico.

▲ Mission Control at the Johnson Space Center in Houston. Mission Control talks to the astronauts in space.

Solve This #7

The table below lists all the space shuttles that have flown and the number of flights for each shuttle.

Space Shuttle	# of Flights
Atlantis	26
Challenger	10
Columbia	28
Discovery	31
Endeavour	19

Math 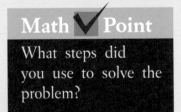 Point

What steps did you use to solve the problem?

What is the average number of flights? (Remember: To find an average, you add the sum of the numbers. Then you divide the sum by the number of addends to find the average.)

How People Have Fun

In the Southwest, people have fun in a lot of ways. They visit famous places and museums. They go to outdoor events.

The Alamo in Texas is a famous place. In 1836, Texas was a part of Mexico. But Texans wanted to be an independent country. An important fight for freedom took place at the Alamo.

The Alamo is in downtown San Antonio. The Spanish built it in 1724 as a mission, a kind of church.

The Buffalo Bill Museum is near Golden, Colorado. Buffalo Bill rode for the Pony Express. He also started a Wild West show in the late 1800s. In the show, people rode horses and did tricks.

▼ On summer nights, millions of bats fly out of Carlsbad Caverns in New Mexico.

▲ Buffalo Bill and his Wild West Show were very popular.

Conclusion

Y ou've just taken a trip to the Southwest. Now you know about the region's geography, climate, and people. You also learned what the region is like today.

The table below can help you remember the states in the Southwest. Use it to help you remember one fact you found out about each state, too.

States in the Southwest

State	Capital
Arizona	Phoenix
Colorado	Denver
New Mexico	Santa Fe
Oklahoma	Oklahoma City
Texas	Austin

Solve This Answers

1. page 5

   269,000 − 197,000 = 72,000 square miles

2. page 9

   a. 13,161 − 70 = 13,091 feet

   b. 14,433 − 13,161 = 1,272 feet

3. page 10

   a. 41 inches

   b. 9–46 inches

4. page 14 Oklahoma (273,230)

   273,230 + 255,879 + 173,483 + 118,362 + 44,241 = 865,195

   865,195 / 5 = 173,039

5. page 19

   a. 1882–1888: 1,500 − 100 = 1,400 decrease in population

   b. Answers will vary.

6. page 22

   Feet to yards: 5,280 / 3 = 1,760 yards

7. page 26

   25 + 9 + 28 + 30 + 19 = 114; 114 / 5 = 22.8 flights

Glossary

adobe
(uh-DOH-bee) a brick made of clay (page 13)

elevation
(eh-luh-VAY-shuhn) the height of a place above or below sea level (page 8)

export
(EK-sport) to send a product to another country (page 24)

festival
(FES-ti-vuhl) a time of celebration (page 21)

gulf
(GULF) a part of the sea or ocean that reaches into land (page 8)

landform
(LAND-fawrm) a feature on Earth's surface, such as a mountain or valley (page 4)

monsoon
(mahn-SOON) a wind that brings heavy rain with it (page 10)

mountain range
(MOWN-tuhn RANJ) a group of mountains that are connected (page 6)

peak
(PEEK) the pointed top of a hill or mountain (page 6)

plain
(PLAYN) a large, flat region covered in grass but with few trees (page 7)

precipitation
(pree-sih-puh-TAY-shuhn) any form of water that reaches Earth, such as rain, snow, and sleet (page 10)

region
(REE-juhn) an area with one or more features that make it different from other areas (page 2)

Index